ABOUT THE AUTHOR

Edward Gore's life in law spanned four decades, from studying it at Balliol College, Oxford to teaching it at The University of Law in London. In between he spent many years as a solicitor specialising in company and commercial law, working at a range of firms including Linklaters and Lovells, and as a partner at Winward Fearson and Howard Kennedy. He had a stint as a company secretary and sole in-house lawyer at Solvera plc. He also served as in-house lecturer at the City law firm Dickson Minto.

First published 2016 by
Coptic Publishing
Office 408, 10 Great Russell Street,
London WC1B 3BQ

A catalogue record for this book is available from the British Library.

Library of Congress Cataloging-in-Publication Data

Gore Edward, 1956 - 2016
So You'd Like to be a Lawyer? What they don't teach you at law school.

ISBN 978-0-9558771-7-9

1. Law: Study and Revision guides.

Printed and bound in Great Britain by Lightning Source

For family and friends

CONTENTS

CONTENTS

SO YOU'D LIKE TO BE A LAWYER?

WHAT THEY DON'T TEACH YOU AT LAW SCHOOL

BY EDWARD GORE

FOREWORD

This book was written for the benefit of anyone contemplating a career in law. It is full of practical advice and common sense. It is refreshingly irreverent and brutally honest. In short, it tells aspiring lawyers what they really ought to know—but are rarely taught.

Edward Gore speaks from experience. For seven years he was himself a teacher at one of London's main colleges of law. Before that he spent 27 years as a practising lawyer, both with firms of solicitors (including Linklaters and Lovells) and as an "in-house" counsel with an industrial company. And he became acutely aware of the yawning gap between the formal training offered to would-be lawyers and the simple savvy needed for the actual practice of law. So he set out to fill that gap. The result is a no-nonsense guide to "what they don't teach you at law school".

Edward was generous in offering words of advice to young people, and nothing would have pleased him more than to see this book help a new generation of lawyers. Alas, he died of cancer before its publication. But his deep, distinctive voice speaks clearly through these pages—a friendly presence offering gentle tips for what can be a daunting profession.

Daniel Franklin
Executive Editor, *The Economist*

INTRODUCTION

So, you'd like to be a lawyer. Perhaps you were inspired by a great film, or literature, or a pivotal moment in history that turned on a courtroom speech or a legal ruling. Perhaps you aspire to play a part in society's unfolding drama yourself. If so, that's all well and good. But remember: before you get a chance to change the world as a lawyer, you will need to navigate years of humdrum routine, office dilemmas, petty competition and much more…and that is where this book may come in handy.

What do I mean by this? For example, imagine, you're at the end of a job interview. It's gone well and you want the job. The interviewer asks what salary you had in mind. Do you name a figure? Or do you suggest the interviewer makes you an offer? Which approach will get you the better deal?

You're daydreaming in the office one morning, when a partner rushes in and tells you to grab your coat — you're off to a meeting. When you arrive, you wonder: What's going on? Who are these people? What am I supposed to do? Indeed, what are you supposed to do?

It's the end of the week and time to file your timesheet. The firm expects 25 chargeable hours a week and you've only done 10. Do you exaggerate to meet your firm's target or record the true time and risk a reprimand or worse for not working hard enough?

These are just some of the everyday dilemmas you will face working as a new lawyer. And your decisions can make or break your career. University and law school teach you all the law you need to know, and a few related skills, but nothing and no-one will prepare you for the practical problems that will confront you. This book aims to help. It will fill these gaping holes and prepare you for the real world of work. Understanding these issues will make a huge difference to your career, from how to land a job to whether you succeed and enjoy the work. So be prepared.

I was a practising solicitor for 27 years and a law tutor

and lecturer for seven. I've seen students, tutors, solicitors and clients up close. My perspective isn't unique but it's given me deeper insights into the real world of the law — insights that I can pass on to you and ease your path through the legal jungle. I may sometimes seem unduly cynical. That's because I'm dealing with what really happens, and one has to be practical, even if it offends.

You will all know that the study and practice of law is becoming costlier, increasingly competitive and ever more demanding. That is unlikely to change in the next few years, if ever. Studying is expensive, it's hard to get a training contract and, even if you do, you still have to survive in a difficult culture and environment.

This book is for those who are considering studying law, those who are already studying it, and those already on a training contract. My advice will be of direct value to any prospective lawyer (though Chapters 4 and 5 may be less relevant to barristers) and useful, indirectly, to prospective professionals in many other fields.

In Chapter 1, we start with the fundamental question of motivation. Chapters 2 and 3 are concerned with studying law at university or college; chapter 4 focuses on applying for, and getting, a training contract. In Chapters 5 and 6, I explore life at a law firm, and the manners and etiquette your colleagues and superiors expect of you. Finally, Chapter 7 considers your first steps as a qualified lawyer and the career options that may open up for you, all the way to partnership.

Learn, enjoy and prosper!

Chapter 1
WHY BECOME A LAWYER?

Money

It's neither the root of all evil nor a pathway to true love, but money is what most lawyers want. Partners in City firms, and Queen's Counsels (QCs), are extremely well paid — as rich as bankers and equally unloved. However, for the majority the picture is less exciting. Most solicitors end up in small firms up and down the country, earning a satisfactory living from such staples as residential conveyancing, probate and legally-aided work on crime. Similarly, most barristers are doing low-grade civil and criminal work in the Magistrates' and Crown Courts, again often legally aided. Spending cuts ate so much into legal-aid funding that in 2014 criminal lawyers went on strike. The well-paid work is in areas such as company and commercial, tax, insurance and major litigation, at the 'magic circle' firms and taken by QCs. They earn at least £100,000. Most of the rest just get by.

In fact, solicitors can no longer take solace from the belief that they will always have work. Getting started is becoming increasingly difficult. Too many solicitors chase too few jobs. Barristers must first find a place in a chambers. Then, like actors or taxi-drivers, they wait to be hired. Instructions come from solicitors to a clerk in the barrister's chambers. The clerk passes the work to whichever barrister he pleases. Although most solicitors will earn a decent living, if you want to become rich from law, think again.

Respect and status

It was the aspiration of many—particularly immigrant— families, that their son or daughter join a profession. It meant they had "arrived". They had achieved the social status that their parents lacked. This is still the case but less so today. For many, lawyers represent greed, obscurantism and pettifogging bureaucracy, and have become the butt of cruel jokes. Of course, such resentments may mask envy. At least, lawyers are thought of as clever, logical and hard-working and usually accorded grudging respect. If status matters to you, the law may be a good career choice.

Pleasing Mum and Dad

My dad has a recurring dream. His doorbell rings, his father is standing there, and my dad asks him: "Am I

doing alright?" Most of us want to please our parents. We may rebel in adolescence but eventually we come round, and this desire to please them continues long after they have died. "Settling down" in an established profession like law is one way of doing so as many parents view happiness as being secure, settled, respected and well-off. But beware! If you become a lawyer just to please them and ignore your own emotions, feelings and talents, you will probably end up deeply unhappy. Go into law only if you think it's right for you.

Your parents may have been or still be lawyers. This has its pros and cons. On the positive side, they will understand the stresses you have to endure and offer wise and sympathetic guidance. Through their contacts, they might help you find a job. Though useful, it could leave you wondering whether you would have made it on your own. On the negative side, it will be difficult to stop comparing yourself with them, leaving you with a deep-seated inferiority complex throughout your career. If neither of your parents are professionals or high-achievers, you might claim to have exceeded their expectations. But they will have little sense for what you're going through and their well-meaning guidance is likely to be uninformed.

A gateway to other careers

Many lawyers leave the law. At some point in their legal careers they decide that law is not for them. It was always thought that the study and practice of law equipped you for other areas of work. You were valued for your organised and logical approach, your problem-solving skills and your verbal and written fluency. The House of Commons is full of ex-lawyers, as are company boardrooms. Nowadays, however, people tend to be pigeonholed much earlier in their careers, so prospective employers outside the law may be unconvinced that you possess the requisite skills and flexibility.

People leave the law at various stages: after graduation or following professional exams, at the end of the training contract, or indeed any time after qualifying as a solicitor.

If you've gone to the time, trouble and expense to pass the exams, you should, at least, complete your training contract or pupillage, and qualify. After all, the exams are the hard bit. Then you only need to tolerate two years as a trainee solicitor, or one year as a barrister's pupil. To leave earlier is, to coin a legal term, a form of *coitus interruptus*.

There are two main ways out of the law. The direct route is to move from a legal practice to a non-law job. This often happens because you're so sick of the law that you can't wait another day to leave. The indirect route is to go 'in-house' first – i.e. as an in-house lawyer or counsel for a manufacturing or services company or organisation, and later to a non-legal role in that organisation. Your legal skills and training give you the initial foot in the door. Alternatively, your law firm might 'second' you to a client where you like it so much that you decide to stay permanently.

So, law may be a stepping stone to bigger and better things. But take note: the typical risk-averse, reactive lawyer tends not to make a great entrepreneur. A partner at Lovells once remarked, not unfairly, that I wasn't much good at getting to the railway station, but once on the track there was no stopping me. This probably applies to many lawyers.

The intellectual challenge
Despite what you read in this book, law can offer you an intellectual challenge. Here are three ways:

Drafting:

The law can be complex and subject to frequent change in the form of new cases, legislation or practices. Your job is to apply the law to your client's circumstances. This involves both knowledge and practical application. Perhaps lawyers' most intellectually challenging task is drafting. This may involve adapting a precedent or drafting from scratch. I always found the latter more interesting, requiring a balance between a full understanding of the client's instructions and the need to fulfil all legal requirements. And it must all be written in clear, plain English. It's a potent mix and you will improve with experience, but you never stop learning.

Negotiating:

In most legal transactions there is the 'other side' to deal with. Whether you're selling or buying a business or a property, or litigating, the terms need to be negotiated. First, you should try to develop a rapport with the other side, though this isn't always possible. Then you must try to be reasonable while continuing to push your client's interests. Third, you may have to negotiate face-to-face with the other side's lawyer. Much has been written about the art of negotiation; all I'll add is that it will stretch your abilities to the full. Like drafting, it will improve with time.

Client management:

The SRA Code of Conduct says that you must 'act in the best interests of your client'. It doesn't say, but it's equally important that you should try to get on with them. This isn't always easy, and if you can't like them then at least reach a tacit understanding and, within reason, follow their instructions. Cultivating good client relationships is essential in a competitive legal world, and can be deeply satisfying, especially when you win repeat business. Some lawyers are naturals, others have to work at it more, but if you can keep the firm's clients happy and attract new business, you will be considered a 'minder and a finder', increasing your partnership chances. By contrast, 'grinders' (i.e. those who just do the hard graft) fare less well.

Altruism and the desire for justice

Believe it or not, there are people who enter the law predominantly to help the less fortunate. They often join small firms specialising in crime, immigration and social-security law. That doesn't necessarily make the rest of us selfish and greedy. Even the least altruistic bring clarity where there is confusion, help clients through difficult periods in their lives, and like a good doctor, are ready, willing and able to help. An ordered society, and all that depends on it, could not function properly without us.

Can't think of anything else to do

Most 17-year-olds, especially 'A' Level arts students, don't know what they want to do in life. They may worry that an interest in history, English, languages or other arts subjects will lead nowhere except perhaps the media or the civil service. The beauty of law, medicine or other professional qualifications is that they light up a clear career path. The problem is that few students study 'A' Level law so are clueless about what they're letting themselves in for.

The best way to resolve this dilemma is consider honestly whether your qualities and skills tally with the needs of a good lawyer. Are you analytical and logical? Do you have an eye for detail? Does your limited knowledge of the law interest you? Do you write and speak well? Can you absorb lots of material quickly? Are you organised? Do you enjoy solving problems? Are you personable and extrovert? If you can answer 'yes' to at least five of these eight questions, the law may well be for you.

The advice of other lawyers is helpful but should not be conclusive. They can provide useful information but their views on your suitability should be taken with a pinch of salt. They bring their own personal prejudices and they don't know you as well as you know yourself!

Finally, and perhaps this should be the ninth question, can you afford it? University and law-school fees, accommodation and living expenses add up. Even if you can borrow all or some of it, you start working life saddled with a large debt. It's a big commitment, which only pays off once you start earning.

Chapter 2
LAW AT UNIVERSITY

If you've won a place at university to study law, you've already done well because, like other vocational subjects, law is extremely popular. Sadly, the days when you could apply to read Sanskrit and change to law after a term have long since gone. The college authorities have got wise to that little manoeuvre. What other experiences await you?

Relevance in practice

Core legal subjects studied at university include British Constitution, Contract, Tort and Criminal. Law at university is not designed to be of practical benefit in your professional life. Its main aim is to get you thinking like a lawyer. You learn how to read primary sources (cases and statutes), secondary sources (textbooks), demonstrate your powers of reasoning and analysis in essays, dissertations and exams, and how to express your-self clearly in tutorials. No doubt, all this is invaluable when practising law. However, the actual substance of what you learn has limited practical value unless, perhaps, you are a litigator. If you want practicality and relevance, you're better off studying another subject alto-gether and applying to a law school afterwards. There is one exception: occasionally, a senior solicitor or partner will ask you to research a particular matter and prepare a memorandum on it that requires you to draw on skills developed at university. But working in the law mostly involves procedure—e.g. how to sell a house or a compa-ny—and here your university studies will be of little use.

The limited value of lectures

Most lecturers are far from inspiring. Often they are bril-liant academics, and would rather be writing books than entertaining undergraduates. You turn up to the first lecture of the first term, bright-eyed and bushy-tailed and full of enthusiasm. The hall is as packed as Old Trafford on a big match day. By week four it's more like a Barnet mid-week game on a wet, winter evening. What happened? First, the lecturer was deathly dull. Second, you just can't be bothered and anyway it's far too early in the morning. Third, you now realise that the lecture materials are in the books anyway. And fourth, you real-ise that attendance is not compulsory. Although some students prefer to hear rather than read the materials, and the rare, charismatic speaker can bring the subject to life, generally the best attended lectures are the revision lectures, where panicky students can get invaluable pre-exam notes.

Tutorials and seminars

It's happened to all of us. The tutorial is tomorrow and you haven't even started on your essay. Once again, there's rising panic, tons of caffeine and pacing the room until 3.00 am. You have a tutorial every week and, like most students, you've deferred the pain until the last minute. And yet, somehow, you always manage to produce something. The fear of not doing your work outweighs the misery of the 'all-nighter'. Paradoxically, this is a good thing. It prepares you for the pressures of work and hones your ability to produce something regardless of the apparent hopelessness of your situation. This is valuable self-knowledge.

The tutor-student ratio varies, from just two students per tutor, to a tutor and a whole classroom. Whatever the ratio, you will either be asked to read your own essay, comment on someone else's or say something about the subject under discussion. Regardless of how many are in the tutorial, you will come under the spotlight even if only briefly. The prospect of public humiliation alone should make you prepare—mirroring life in practice. Tutorials have other benefits. The tutor is knowledge-able and worth listening to. His enthusiasm may be infectious. Even a poor lecturer may flourish in a more intimate tutorial. And the student gets the chance to ask questions and get helpful answers.

But tutorials also have pitfalls. Your fellow students may be 'stummers' — that is they say little, forcing you to expound more than you'd like. Then there are moments of terrifying silence, particularly after you've given an unsatisfactory answer. A distant clock chimes, birds tweet and a desperate rustling of notes can be heard. They're all waiting for you to say something but you've got nothing to say. It's horrific, but you'll survive. If you meet your tutors in later life you'll laugh about it, though it wasn't funny at the time.

University tutors regard the law as an academic subject. Tutors at law colleges (e.g. The University of Law, BPP) see it as a vocational subject. University tutors train their students to be academics whereas law college tutors understand their students' wish is to qualify. These conflicting approaches explain why at university you must consider such questions as "What reforms would you suggest to the law in Foss v Harbottle?" or "Is the current law for compensating the victims of accidents adequate?" The trouble with this approach is that you usually have just one week to bone up on the actual law and then you have to suggest reforms to it.

I found it hard enough just to learn the relevant law in the time given without also having to opine on its fitness, and longed for my tutor simply to explain the law to me, which they clearly felt was unnecessary. It seemed somewhat premature to give an opinion on the future of laws which you didn't understand in the first place. No doubt this approach suited the brightest students; but I felt out of my depth and so, I'm sure, many of you will too.

Memorising and regurgitating

Throughout your career you will have to absorb a lot of material very quickly and then use that knowledge with

clients and your opposite number. Law at university prepares you well for this. You will usually have a week to learn about a particular legal area. This involves reading the relevant materials, discussing them at your tutorial, and writing about them in exams—the same process as in practice. As a result, most lawyers have good short-term, if less than wonderful long-term, memories. There are exceptions. Some lawyers can remember in great detail transactions they worked on five years earlier and even recall particular provisions. I don't believe you can train yourself to have a good long-term memory, and you can't fake it. These lawyers tend to get the first-class degrees and shoot up the partnership ranks. I think you've either got it or you haven't.

But we mortals do at least acquire a good short-term memory through studying law, and we retain this for the rest of our careers.

Boredom and anxiety

Studying law at university involves a rare combination of boredom and anxiety: boredom because so much dull material has to be learned; and anxiety arising from essay crises, the volume of material to be learned, and an intensely competitive job market ahead. However, like memorising and regurgitating, your course will prepare you well for practice, where you will strive to satisfy clients, impress partners, meet deadlines, and climb the partnership ladder. Still, doing well, receiving rare praise from tutors, and ending up with a good degree can be exhilarating or at least satisfying. May this exceed the stress in your case!

Colleagues and cliques

"A pride of lions." "A gaggle of geese." "A flock of swans." And a "clique" of lawyers, perhaps? From early on at university, you and your legal contemporaries will stick together—a bond that can last a lifetime. Although you probably won't like them all, these ties are mysterious. Like the infamous chant of Millwall football fans, "No-one loves us, we don't care", lawyers develop a strange unity that derives from their distinctive and often unloved persona within wider society. These ties form early on, and persist through life as you monitor your peers' progress in exams, job applications and careers.

Pros and cons of qualifying

If you get a law degree, and then want to qualify, you have to do the Legal Practice Course ('LPC') for around one year or take the accelerated course that lasts seven months. Fees in London were about £15,000 for 2016. If you have a non-law degree, you have to do the GDL (Graduate Diploma in Law) for one year, followed by the LPC. GDL fees in London were in the region of £10,500. Either way, it's a major financial commitment even after taking into account the various scholarship and sponsorship possibilities. And the cost comes on top of debts you may already have built up at university.

Therefore, once you've completed your degree you need to think hard about whether you want to go on to qualify. Here are some pros and cons to consider:

Pros:

1. You will be the solicitor or barrister that you set out to be.
2. For those with a law degree, you've already done half the job.
3. Having spent a fortune already, only by practising will you repay it.
4. You enjoy the law and actually want to qualify.

Cons:

1. You've studied law and it's not for you.
2. You can't take another year or two of intensive study.
3. You can't afford it.

It's a difficult decision but, if at all possible, I would urge you to qualify. If you give up, you may regret it for the rest of your life.

Chapter 3
SURVIVING LAW SCHOOL

Which law school?

The U.K.'s three main law schools are: The University of Law, BPP and Kaplan. There are also increasing numbers of institutions offering legal professional courses.

If you have an English law degree and want to practise law, then you must study either the Legal Practice Course ('LPC'), for solicitors, or the Bar Professional Training Course ('BPTC'), for barristers. Both take one year but some of the legal firms may require prospective trainees to do the LPC in seven months, known as the 'Accelerated' LPC. In London the LPC currently costs as much as £15,000 and the BPTC £19,000.

If you have a non-law degree, prospective solicitors and barristers must do the Graduate Diploma in Law ('GDL') before taking the LPC or the BPTC respectively. This one-year course costs around £10,500 in London. So, if you don't have a law degree you have two years of intensive study ahead of you at a combined maximum cost of almost £30,000.

These courses consist of workshops (with around 20 students) and lectures (usually many more). The former are far more important. Like university tutorials, you have to prepare and participate, and issues covered form the core of the final exams. My earlier comments about university lectures also apply to those at law college. You will be required to prepare for each workshop by reading specified materials from a text book, statutory extracts and, occasionally, cases. You are also given i-tutorials (computerised talks) to view.

The LPC year is divided into two roughly equal, terms—the compulsories and the electives. Compulsory subjects on the LPC are: Business, Property and Litigation and other subjects grouped under the heading "skills" (i.e. interviewing, advocacy, solicitors' accounts, legal writing and legal drafting).

The GDL consists of the basics: Contract, Tort, Land and Public Law. The GDL is slightly more academic than the LPC but both are precise and prescriptive compared with law at university.

When the tutors mark your final exams, they will have 'Points to Note' for each question, allocating marks for each accurate point made.

Some law colleges now have the power to award law degrees, so you can, for example, get an LLB at the University of Law or, if you are more academically inclined, an LLM.

Law schools want you. You are the customer, and there's fierce competition for your business. As long as you satisfy the basic requirements, you are in. Several factors will determine your choice:

Reputation:

The best people to ask are the recent graduates. Their memories will be fresh and clear. But if possible, visit the place to see if you like it. The University of Law and BPP are safe choices, but remember, the law firm you eventually join won't care as long as you've passed the LPC.

Cost:

The costs don't vary much. Some schools will let you pay by instalments and may offer scholarships or awards. If you have already obtained a training contract your firm may tell you which college to attend and pay your tuition costs and living expenses (you lucky devil!)

If self-financing, remember to factor in living costs. Some law colleges offer accommodation, or you may be able to live with your family. But a long commute can be tedious as well as costly.

Lifestyle:

Also, would you prefer city life or a small town? Whatever your choice, don't wait till the last minute. Unless you are taking a year off after university, you have between June and September to get sorted. So, start working on it in July.

The firm's requirements

Most large law firms offer training contracts before the LPC starts, and specify which law college you must attend. The firm will tell you what law-school courses you should do in your Electives (2nd term) and very often the law school will have designed those courses in conjunction with that firm. So you will probably attend the same workshop as your future colleagues, which can be positive, but also means that the competition kicks off early.

Genius not required

Geniuses at university often do well at law school. Fortunately for the average student, this doesn't always follow. Academia celebrates the ability to question, criticise and come up with novel arguments. This is of no use whatsoever at law school. The vast majority of employers only require you to pass (i.e. 50%), not win a commendation (60%-70%) or a distinction (70%). So, what do you need to get through? Being organised is essential. The work comes thick and fast. Get yourself some good lever-arch files and subdivide them logically. Take notes at workshops and lectures. Work in a disciplined way. Indeed, treat it like an office job with set hours and proper concentration. Decide early on whether you work better at home, in the library, or a combination of both. In other words, establish a work pattern and stick to it. You will need physical and mental stamina for the GDL and LPC. So, balance work and play, set a daily target and stick to it. This might sound obvious, but keep fit and well. You will need your physical strength to get through.

Part-time jobs

Many students have part-time jobs. I try to discourage this, if financially possible. The GDL and LPC are full-time occupations and leisure time should be just that.

This advice also applies to internships or other law-office work. Now is not the time to gain a commercial advantage. Students can be under tremendous financial pressure but working more than 3 nights a week will jeopardise your career.

Falling behind

Work at law school is like an avalanche. There's lots of it, and it picks up weight and speed with incredible rapidity. If you fall behind by a week, you can probably make up the lost time. But losing two or more weeks can land you in trouble. Falling behind leads to anxiety and panic. So, don't leave everything to the last minute, and organise your time efficiently and effectively. Don't try and absorb every last detail at this stage. There will be time for that during the revision period. But first and foremost, make sure you understand the material—and be honest with yourself about this. I frequently come across students who have memorised the detail but haven't grasped the principles. Rote learning won't do. Understanding comes first, detail later.

Nevertheless, you might find yourself asking prob-
ing questions: Why am I studying law? Why am I doing
these exams? Is this particular law fair? Don't. At university you are encouraged to think 'outside the box' and to
question the purpose of, or reform to, a particular piece
of law. None of this is of any use during your professional exams and should be discouraged.

Specified materials only

Each week you will be told exactly what to read for each
subject. It is usually a combination of textbook, statutes
and i-tutorial (i.e. webinars). Sometimes optional, additional reading is mentioned, but not strictly necessary. If
you follow these instructions to the letter, you will pass
the exams with ease and often with a commendation or a
distinction. There is absolutely no need to read anything
else. Unlike university, where intellectual exploration
is encouraged, reading around your subject is not only
unnecessary but may distract you from the essentials.
Studying the prescribed materials is quite enough. Don't
be a bigger swot than necessary.

Stating the obvious

Exam questions will inevitably comprise factual scenar-
ios to which you are asked to apply the relevant law in
advising the client. If there is a law-college mantra, it's:

"Apply the law to the facts". It's what you will do in practice and is therefore particularly relevant to the LPC. The trouble with this approach is that it can seem blindingly obvious. But say it anyway. As Basil in the TV series *Fawlty Towers* was fond of saying, "Special Subject: The Bleeding Obvious". For example, in company law you learn that the requisite quorum for a board meeting is stated in the company's articles and is usually two. Jack and Jill are both directors. So, say that if they attend the board meeting they will constitute a quorum. It may seem trite and obvious to you but it must be said.

Participation

You, or someone on your behalf, have paid for you to do the GDL or LPC. You might think that entitles you to attend as many or as few workshops and lectures as you want, but you'd be wrong. First, you might as well use all the resources that the College has to offer. Second, if the law firm is paying, they will expect you to attend regularly, and can check. Third, and perhaps most importantly, regular attendance will give your working week a structure and purpose and let you mark your progress. And if your teacher's easy questions leave you flummoxed, it's a sign that you haven't fully understood the topic. Finally, as pack animals, we need company, and regular attendance prepares you for the collaborative nature of working in the law. If you have to, it's better to miss a lecture than a workshop.

Get organised

Good organisation consists of the following:

1. Have well-organised lever-arch files for each subject. Sub-divide these for each area within that subject. Keep all relevant materials and your notes there. This will prove invaluable when it comes to revision. I know it's a pain (literally) humping heavy files around but it pays off and will get you in shape for all the heavy lifting you will have to do as a trainee.

2. When not attending workshops or lectures, decide where to work. College is sociable, it has a library and it helps structure your day. Provided

you can resist the gossip, it's better than working at home. But only you can decide where you work best.

3. Prepare for workshops in good time. Dump the university all-nighters. Create a weekly work plan and stick to it. But leave yourself some 'down-time' in the evening. This is a marathon not a sprint, so pace yourself like a long-distance athlete.

4. As the dreaded exams approach, you will be tempted to make copious notes. They should be as concise as possible, particularly if they are allowed in the exam itself. The very act of paring down is also an invaluable way to declutter the mind.

The 7- or 12-month LPC

The LPC normally lasts 12 months. However, there is now a seven-month option, which some large solicitors' firms require of prospective trainees. The cost is the same but large firms with contracts with BPP and the University of Law introduced this to get their trainees working quicker. And given that they're also paying your living expenses, they want to control costs. So, if you have a training contract with one such firm you will have no choice in the matter.

Otherwise, why put yourself under unnecessary pressure? The LPC is hard enough, and you will discover what intolerable pressure is like when you start work.

Firm specific

Another recent innovation at BPP and the University of Law is to divide workshops into 'specific' and 'non-specific' groups. There is a simple reason for this and, as with the seven-month LPC, it is driven by the large firms. Many will have agreed with BPP or the University of Law to send their prospective trainees to one or the other. In return, they want those students to sit together in separate classes ('the firm specifics') and to benefit from tailor-made courses. For their part, the law colleges enjoy large fee income and are happy to oblige. As with the seven-month LPC, you will have no choice in the matter. But this has drawbacks. It creates a class system that can make the firm specifics feel slightly superior. It narrows your social life. And it forces people to measure themselves against their peers, creating additional and pointless tensions. However, with no choice, moaning is futile (though I just have on your behalf).

Chapter 4
APPLYING FOR A TRAINING CONTRACT

It used to be so simple. Flick through *The Legal 500* and pick some firms, send out your CV plus covering letter and wait for the interview. There was no set format—just a gentle conversation with a partner or two. And then, if you're lucky, a job offer. There were no online application forms, internships or vacation schemes to worry about. During my training contract interview, a senior partner popped his head round the door, asked me my name, thought for a bit, and then said: "I know your Uncle Simon. Charming man. You've got the job. Just make sure you pass your exams."

But enough reminiscing! Anyone who wants to qualify as a solicitor in England and Wales has to spend two years working in a law office, usually after completing the LPC. In my opinion, by now the hard part has already been done; you just have to survive what is effectively a compulsory apprenticeship. Only illness, injury, serious misconduct or giving up can stop you.

Applying for this two-year training contract, however, is much more complicated nowadays. But the following tips might help.

Finding potential employers

First, you need to decide whether you want to do your training in London or elsewhere. If you're fascinated by a particular area of law then only apply to firms that specialise in it. Then decide if you're going for the big firms (i.e. with 200+ partners), mid-tier (50-200 partners), smaller operations, or a mix of all three. The best place to obtain detailed information about each firm, and how to apply is the lawcareers.net website. Also look at: *The Training Contract and Pupillage Handbook*; the *Chambers Student Guide*; *The Legal 500* and *The Lex 100*. There's no shortage of written information on training contracts.

Online applications

Most large firms require online applications—check the publications listed above. This time-consuming exercise takes about two days. But if you're applying while studying, then consider how much time is worth spending on it. If you only have the time to do three, then look for additional firms that only require a covering letter plus CV.

Degrees

I'd like to deny it, but a good degree does make the application process easier. Indeed, some firms require a 2:1 or higher. Others state only that a 2:1 + is "preferred". But don't despair if you fall short. Firms may consider counter-balancing factors—like achieving a distinction or commendation in the GDL or LPC, relevant work experience, or a prolonged illness—in which case your applications should emphasise this. There may be other mitigating factors, but normally a 2:2 or a third minimises your chances with larger firms (though a prestigious university might help). Generally, be realistic and apply to mid-tier or smaller firms.

Timing

Traineeship applications usually have an end-July deadline for a September start two years later. Though some smaller firms may have a shorter start period, it means that you need to think about training while still at university. Like everything in law, you have to be organised.

CV and covering letter

Many, usually small- or mid-tier, firms are more traditional, requiring only a CV and covering letter. But each letter must be tailored to each firm. For example, if one specialises in family law, say why you're interested in family issues and mention any relevant work experience. Most law colleges now have "employability" services that can help with the form and content of your letters. Unless firms specify otherwise, you should type the letter; also check if you should email or post it.

In-house or Alternative Business Structures

Many large non-law organisations in all fields, from retailing to banking, have their own legal department and hire trainees. It's worth checking that their trainee-ships have been approved by the Solicitors Regulation Authority. There are also traineeships with governmental organisations and local authorities.

The advantage of training in-house is that it allows you to get involved in your area of interest immediately, though it may lack the breadth of training available in a law firm. Also, it is fair to say that early on in your career it is harder to switch from in-house to law firm than vice versa. Furthermore, in-house lawyers rarely reap the handsome financial rewards enjoyed by a law partner. Given the choice, I would, on balance, pick the law firm.

Alternative Business Structures—law firms owned by non-lawyers or where the non-lawyers have an interest of 10% or more—have been legal since 2007. These will become more common in time, but it's probably too early to judge their value to a trainee.

Play to your strengths not your connections

Think carefully about what might distinguish you application in this intensely competitive market. If you speak
fluent Spanish, for example, target Spanish firms in
London, or firms with Spanish or Latin American offices.

Now we come to the contentious issue of "connections".
The shameful word that dares not speak its name implies
nepotism and favouritism—and is frowned-upon in our
meritocratic age. And yet the habit persists, if covert-
ly. Perhaps you are related to the managing director of
a client company, or to a firm's partner. But be subtle
about exploiting the connection. Certainly never refer
to it in letters or documents. At an appropriate juncture,
probably during the interview, you may refer to your
connection in an offhand way, as if it were of no impor-
tance. If your "connection" is already known before the
interview I wouldn't refer to it at all. What could be an
advantage can all too easily backfire spectacularly.

Work experience

A valuable start is to gain an internship "vac" scheme
at a firm where you wish to train. These typically take
place in the summer and last a week or two. Many firms
appoint their trainees from their own vac schemes and so
they are important and, inevitably, difficult to get.

There are other types of valuable work experience: for
example, a vac scheme at another firm; 'pro bono' work
in the legal field (demonstrating social responsibility); or

non-legal work at a high-street solicitor.

All in all, you are trying to present yourself as someone who is not just academically able but also has some real-world experience, legal or otherwise.

So, at the risk of repeating myself, work experience is vital.

The offer and salary

Many U.S. firms have opened London offices and admit trainees. With starting salaries as high as £40,000, the students are worked very hard. But I doubt it's tougher there than in any of the top five, so called 'magic circle' London law firms. More importantly, U.S. and other foreign firms in London may have different working cultures. If the legal staff are mainly from the home country, you may feel excluded, something you can only judge once you're there.

The range of starting salaries for trainees is wide – from just £15,000 annually to £40,000. But don't let money rule your decision. There's no saying what you might eventually earn in what should be a long career. Other factors, such as an interest in your work, growth of the practice and your relationship with colleagues, are more important.

It is rare for job offers to be conditional on you getting a Commendation or Distinction in the LPC. Most firms simply want you to pass the exams and be ready to start work on the appointed day. In fact, your academic performance will pale into insignificance in time, and what will matter most will be your career profile.

Apply to as many firms as you can. If you're invited for interview, go. The firm in question may not appeal much, but you need the interview practice. And who knows, you may turn out to be wrong about the firm.

Most firms will want to interview you at least twice. The first may be by phone, or with the Human Resources department. Alternatively, it may take the entire day and take place with all the other short-listed applicants. Every firm is different. Interviews may feel informal (usually with smaller firms) or be tightly scripted. Be prepared for all possibilities.

Does size matter?

Many students believe that only mega firms in the City of London (with 200 or more partners) really count and they therefore only apply to such firms for a training contract. This is a mistake. There are hundreds of other firms which might suit you better. As well as being hard to get into, the mega firms can feel impersonal, and you will have little client contact. And they might just spit you out at the end of your traineeship. Even if, despite all that, they still appeal, don't put all your eggs in one basket. Of course, the big players appeal to our vanity, not least because they are an impressive name for your CV. But consider whether this, and the benefits of a good salary and impressive client experience, outweighs the disadvantages. In truth, it probably does; and the fact is you rarely hear of anyone declining a mega firm's training contract.

The provinces and boutique firms

'The provinces' is what we city lawyers patronisingly call anywhere outside London. Aspiring young lawyers seem just as fixated with London as with mega firms. But firms in the provinces are just as varied as those in the capital. They range from one-man bands in small market towns to large, commercial firms in Birmingham, Manchester

THE MAGIC CIRCLE

or Leeds. They may even be so-called 'national' firms with offices in several English towns. All of life is here, so don't ignore it! These firms know that they are not always a candidate's first, second or even third choice so make it clear in your application that's not how you see them. Stress a particular reason why you want to go to that place (e.g. family or university connection). London is an expensive and stressful place to work and is not for everybody.

'Boutique' firms are small and specialise in a particular area of law. They have all the pros and cons of small firms – knowing everyone, early responsibility, rapid advancement and so on. However, working in one can be problematic if you don't fit in early on. These firms are good for those who know what area of law they want to practise. But, if it turns out to be wrong, then you're stuck. So it may be better to join them once you've qualified.

Exams and training contract applications are the hard part. The traineeship is the home straight – with money finally coming in and only two years to get through.

Chapter 5
LIFE AS A TRAINEE

You've got your training contract and the day of reckoning has arrived. You turn up on the first day, appropriately suited and booted. Now you are faced with a new set of issues and challenges and the purpose of this chapter is to alert you to these.

Appearance

You can't judge a book by its cover but people still do. Law is a conventional and conservative profession. Keep your sartorial flamboyance and eccentricity for outside the office. Copy other senior lawyers in the firm. If that's difficult to gauge, then stick to the following basic rules.

For men, wear dark (black, grey or navy) suits, white or blue shirts and reasonably sober ties (if worn at the firm). Invest in a good pair of black shoes, preferably brogues or half-brogues. Definitely no jewellery (except cufflinks) or, heaven forbid, face piercings or tattoos (although it may be a little late to remove the latter). Have at least two or three suits, and avoid flashy style features such as overflowing handkerchief in breast pocket, double-breasted suits (if single–breasted is the current convention) or excess jacket pockets. Keep all clothes and shoes clean and fresh.

Ties can be an issue. In many firms ties are only worn in the presence of clients. Just follow what everyone else does. And please no ties at half-mast like a second-division footballer! Either top button done up and tie firmly in place or, where appropriate, no tie.

Some firms operate a 'dress-down Friday' policy. This is not an invitation to wear jeans, T-shirt and old trainers. It's really unwritten code for blazer, chinos, good casual shirt and loafers. This can be particularly difficult for men who have long benefited from the simple uniformity of the suit.

Pay attention to your hairstyle. Too severe and you may resemble the client that you've just sprung from jail. But long hair or excessively trendy haircuts are not on either. Keep it neat, well-groomed and, above all, conventional. The same applies to facial hair. Many of my students are half-shaven. In the office, either be clean-shaven or have a well-groomed beard or moustache.

Rules for women (and here I draw on the views of a sensible female colleague) are similar to those for men. Black, navy or dark grey suits and, in most firms, trousers as part of a suit. No extreme hairstyles or hair colours and understated, low-key jewellery. Shirt or top—any colour, within reason—a smart work bag, and shoes one can walk in, are advised. In short, rely on your own good dress sense and good quality.

Being cheerful and enthusiastic

As they grow older solicitors get jaded and cynical. It's an occupational hazard. To a certain extent they rely on trainees to restore their faith. Trainees have little to offer in terms of expertise and experience but they are still young, relatively cheerful and optimistic. This can be a welcome tonic for older solicitors and they will be grateful for it. So, look happy and be keen and enthusiastic. When you are given work to do, look and sound pleased, regardless of your true feelings. Walk around the office with a spring in your step. As a separate but related matter, your general knowledge of the law should be more up to date than theirs and you will find that your supervisors often refer to this. Keep your university/GDL and LPC notes with you in the office. You'll be surprised how useful they can be in practice. Always show willingness to research law for your supervisor. Nowadays, your GDL and LPC training includes certain 'skills'—advocacy, interviewing etc. However, in practice, your supervisor won't look to you for these skills. What they will expect, however, is that you know the law and that you are cheerful and enthusiastic about this wonderful new world. Now, don't go too far with this. Incessant grinning lacks 'gravitas' even for a trainee, and will be irritating.

Reliability

You're asked to draft a letter, a file note or a memorandum for your supervisor. It's Monday and he or she tells you he must have it by Friday. The number one rule here is: no matter how good, bad or indifferent your work may be you must give it to him on time. Being late with work is a cardinal sin. If you get a reputation for being unreliable, that reputation sticks and news travels fast among partners and supervisors. You may never be trusted again. The same principle applies to other forms of reliability. Being asked or volunteering to do something by a certain time either for your supervisor or the client and then not delivering on time is unforgiveable. There are two potential problems here. You may be given an unfeasibly short time to do something. If so, speak now or forever hold your peace. As in my earlier example, don't tell your supervisor or client on Thursday that you can't deliver on Friday. Similarly, if you already have too much work and simply cannot take on another project, then say so early. If two or more supervisors need your help at the same time and you cannot manage both, it's for them to sort it out between them, although don't go so far as to suggest this.

Perfectionism is an admirable quality but not at the expense of reliability and punctuality. If necessary, you may have to sacrifice quality and to qualify your work by saying that you haven't had the time to consider a certain issue or issues. If your supervisor doesn't like that, it's just too bad. To make you feel better, you will often be given unrealistic deadlines because either your supervisor is thoughtless or he has been trying to impress the client—at your expense—with his or the firm's excellent, prompt service. You are not to blame but you mustn't ignore the issue even if that means incurring your supervisor's wrath.

Some deadlines are immoveable. A deal is closing or a claim has to be issued by a particular time. In those circumstances you just have to lump it. Or, to quote Rowan Atkinson's headmaster sketch, "Yes, Undermanager, isn't life tragic!".

Mistakes

Fears of mistakes or negligence stalk every lawyer. We all make them and we all dread them. It's one reason why lawyers are risk averse. Serious negligence can severely damage a reputation and even end a career. If you are lucky, your mistakes won't be noticed or will be minor, resulting in little loss. It's a difficult balance to strike: too afraid of being wrong, your opinions will be so heavily qualified as to be almost worthless; but be too cavalier or broad brush, and trouble awaits. Clients pay you to be right and decisive. You can't be both.

Mistakes can, of course, be much more straightforward. For example, the law is full of time limits such as registering a charge within a specified time or filing a claim by a certain date. If you mess this up, you have no defence. So you must get into the habit of keeping a diary for registering important dates. Lawyers live by lists. Being organised is as important as being clever. I make a list every day of things I had to do that day. Anything not done gets carried forward to the next day. This reduces the chance of missing something important. If you realise that you have made a mistake or given poor or negligent advice, never brush it under the carpet and hope it will go away. First, it probably won't. Second, when you finally 'confess' to your supervisor, he will be furious because your delay may have made matters worse. Remember, your supervisor takes the blame from the client, colleagues or partners. Finally, by not coming clean quickly it looks like you put your interests before the firm's. As a trainee, never admit a mistake or negligence to the client. Always discuss it with your supervisor first.

It all sounds gloomy but don't be discouraged. This is part of professional life—and the sooner you accept it the better. Also remember that all solicitors' firms have professional indemnity insurance against negligence claims, so it is rare for your mistake to cost the firm or its clients.

Asking questions

As a trainee, and for the rest of your legal career, you will have to ask colleagues and supervisors for help—and the less experienced you are, the more you will need to ask. It is tempting to call on the person closest to hand, who may find your questions irritating or stupid. But if that person happens to be a partner, bombarding him or her with questions not only will create a bad impression that is hard to eradicate, it may harm your long-term prospects.

So, what should you do? First, be selective: where possible, ask people nearer your own age and seniority. They're more likely to be sympathetic, having dealt with similar issues themselves not so long ago. More importantly, they are less able to damage your promotion prospects. Partners and senior solicitors are usually busy people and may feel you are wasting their valuable time, no matter how sensible your question may be. So cultivate good relations with your contemporaries and those slightly above you…. which brings us to another complex issue.

Favours

Here is a rule of life not just of traineeships. You know how angry you feel when your good turn isn't reciprocated or even acknowledged. The same applies in the office. If someone does you a favour, be sure to acknowledge and remember it, and when the opportunity arises, do the same for them. Not only is this basic good manners, it is also in your best interests. If you don't remember a favour done, the offended person certainly will, and will be sure not to help again. Acknowledge small favours in writing; for major favours, a gift—lunch, flowers, chocolates, etc—is appropriate. As they say, "what goes around comes around".

Remembering the troops

As with favours, it's all too easy to focus solely on other solicitors in your firm. But others must be considered—such as secretaries, the IT help team, the print room, the accounts department and Reception, to name just a few. They can be crucial to the smooth and timely operation of a transaction, and you will surely need them, especially at times of great stress. And at a purely personal level, it can be a pleasure to speak to people other than solicitors or clients. So, you can have some fun and do the right thing. I dated a woman from the print department for two years. So you never know where a friendly approach can lead.

Bluffing

Consider the scenario, set out in the book's introduction. A partner asks you, last minute, to come to a meeting. She briefs you in the taxi, but you're not much the wiser. Once there, you don't know who anyone is. There are no introductions, and you'll be lucky to receive any business cards. Then, as the meeting begins the partner leans over and asks you to take the meeting notes. Help! Who are our clients? Who's the fat bloke in the corner? What are they talking about? If you can write fast enough (which is unlikely) your note can be a verbatim account of proceedings. If you're lucky, nobody will pay much attention to your note. But you could find yourself horribly exposed. When you return to the office, your best bet is to talk to another solicitor involved in the issue to help make sense of it. The point is, beware of this trap the moment you are asked to attend a meeting. And then just hope for the best!

Jacket on back of the chair

Bluffing doesn't happen just in meetings. The perfect employee arrives early, skips lunch and works late. More importantly, he wants to be seen to do these things, and may rely on artifice to impress the boss. But does the jacket-on-the-chair routine actually work? Whether it does or not, unorthodox hours tend to work against you. It can be infuriating when little happens during normal office hours, but then everything kicks off at 5pm, and you are forced into yet another late night. Unfortunately, this is the world you're joining and it is assumed that everyone loves to work all hours.

Time differences are one cause of this problem. Americans don't get busy until mid-afternoon London time (later if they're on the West Coast). And with Far Eastern colleagues or clients, you have to get to the office at the crack of dawn.

Much also depends on the location of your desk. If you're by the main door, you can slip in and out unnoticed; that's not so easy if you have to run the gauntlet of partners' rooms. You'll just have to appear particularly resolute as if en route to an important meeting.

Heading out early is less of an obstacle in summer, when you don't need a coat so no-one knows if you're leaving the building. If there is a choice, it's better stay late than get in early. The late worker is likely to elicit more admiration. Similarly, do not return late from lunch unless you've been with a client or partner.

This advice may seem trivial but, unfortunately, such things do make a difference.

Timesheets

You have to prepare timesheets every day and then, depending on your firm's requirements, file them either daily or at the end of each week. Your timesheet records how many hours you've spent on each matter. That total is then multiplied by your hourly charge-out rate so that the partner on the case can either review the work-in-progress to date on a particular matter or render a bill to the client.

It is now the practice at some firms for trainees and solicitors to be required to do a certain specified number of chargeable hours per day, week or year. That then raises the almost unanswerable question: what if you haven't actually done the requisite number of hours? Do you overstate your hours (which is fraudulent) or risk reprimand from the partners? I see only one, practical answer to this terrible dilemma. If you're not busy, email all the partners in the department saying so and ask for more work.

Volunteering

There are times when you haven't got enough work. It's tempting just to sit around and do nothing. I considered quiet times to be the perfect opportunity to arrive late, have a long lunch and leave early. But it would have been far better to earn some brownie points by asking a partner in your department if you can help with anything. This will definitely go down well.

Specialising

Assuming you are with a sizeable commercial firm, your two-year traineeship is likely to be spent working in four separate departments, known as "seats", for consecutive six-months periods. The purpose of this is to give you a rounded training. Typically, three of those four seats will be in the corporate/commercial, property and litigation/dispute resolution departments. The fourth will

depend on the firm's other specialisms, e.g. tax, insurance, employment, banking etc. Normally, as you start
your fourth seat, the firm will let you know whether they
intend to offer you a job and in what department, or "let
you go" at the end of your training contract. Depending
on the firm's practice and your perceived strengths and
abilities, you may even be asked which departments you
might want to work in.

This raises some important points:

1. Avoid preconceived notions about where to specialise.
    You may have hated property law on the LPC
    but enjoy it in practice. You may think you have to
    be aggressive to be a litigator but find that a more
    mild temperament works just as well. Six months is
    a relatively short time in one department. It takes
    about three months just to find your feet before you
    start thinking about the next department. Yet this will
    be one of your most crucial career decisions. Wait
    about 18 months into your training contract before
    making a decision, and keep an open mind.

2. Other factors may determine your choice of
    specialism. Your relationship with the other
    solicitors in the department can be a factor. There
    are also tactical considerations. If none of the
    trainees liked Tax, that department might provide the
    better opportunities. What are your firm's strengths?
    Do you like the prevailing culture? Do you fit in?

3. It may be that you are a star at your firm and you like them and they like you. If not, then within about six months of the end of your traineeship you should apply to other firms. Even if your current firm makes you an offer, it's good to have other offers, if only to compare starting salaries.

4. Legal practice is becoming increasingly specialised. It's getting much harder to be a Jack of several trades. It's rare nowadays for firms to allow you to specialise in one area for a few years and then switch to something else. Once you have specialised for, say, a couple of years, it will be difficult to change.

5. You may think longer-term, to the day you move out of law altogether, and into, say, banking, in which case, specialise in banking law. If you fancy yourself as a future captain of industry, do company law. Most of us, however, don't think so far ahead.

Overseas offices

Many large solicitors' firms have overseas offices, and you may have a chance to work at one during your train-eeship. If so, grab it. It shows you as outward-looking and keen to help. It can also be great fun and an experience to remember. If offered a choice, I would go either for an English-speaking country or one where you're likely to develop a good social life.

Partners

Partners can make or break you. They decide whether you are kept on at the end of your training contract, what work you are allocated, your pay increases and, eventually, whether you too are made a partner. Of course, colleagues, non-legal staff and clients also matter, but none so much as partners. Your exposure to the partners may be limited, especially at large firms where at an early career stage you're more likely to be working for other solicitors. Also, others' opinion of you will be considered. However, contact with partners is precious. All your tact, skill and diplomacy must be brought to bear. Sometimes a partner just doesn't like you for reasons you can do nothing about. But, if there's just one lesson in this book, it's that partners matter most.

It's only two years

A training contract is not a life sentence. If you're unhappy at the firm, working for a horrible partner or you just don't fit in, there is a future at the end of your training contract, elsewhere. Even if things are going tolerably well, ask yourself if it's really the firm for you. If you're not sure, then get interviews with other firms in good time before your training contract ends.

Chapter 6
MANNERS

I'm 57. You're probably younger. A generation gap exists, has always existed and always will. In the 1960s music, fashion, hair, drugs and sexual morality divided the generations. Now, I contend, it's manners, behaviour and technology. You will be working with older people, and you cannot allow those differences to harm your working relationships.

What you do in private is your business. I would not even try to influence you. But you do need to know what grates on the older generation—which is why I've included this chapter.

Punctuality
When you're young, poor punctuality is often tolerated and can be amusing. As you get older it becomes irritating and this habit of your youth must be discarded.

So you'd like to be a lawyer?

Although I have already mentioned this, it cannot be stressed enough. Essentially, there are two types of punctuality: meetings and deadlines. For the former, always be slightly early. It is a courtesy and you won't be flustered or disorganised when the meeting starts. Always allow for transport delays, particularly in London. As to getting your work in on time, again, it's more important to get it in than get it absolutely right. Perfectionism is admirable but in business punctuality is essential. If you're going to be late, say so as soon as possible. And finally, never, ever keep a partner waiting for anything. She will never forgive you.

Shaving

As a tutor, I see many unshaven or half-shaven men. Either they can't be bothered to shave or it's the fashion. Either way, it won't be tolerated in practice. The older generation will think you look scruffy or that you don't care about your appearance. This is another example of having to "put aside childish things" and conform. Get a good razor and shave every morning. It may be dreary and conformist but again, there is no choice.

Like y'know, whatever....

Language unites and divides. Every new generation has words or phrases which bond them and exclude the older generation. Use them with your friends and contemporaries but not with your elders, otherwise you risk alienating or irritating them. Here are some of the more grating examples:

"Like" –
As in "I'm like I want to go and see a film and he's like he doesn't want to". Very easy. Substitute "say or said" for "like" and, hey presto, the older generation will understand you.

"Y'know" –
A meaningless conversational filler that lets your brain catch up. I remember when a nervous general election candidate spoke at our school, and all we could do was count the "y'knows". The content was lost. "Y'know" distracts, annoys and reduces the speaker's impact.

"Whatever" –
Another filler, it is exclusively a young person's habit that indicates boredom. So, it is both meaningless and rude.

"Isn't it" (or worse, "Init") –
A catch-all reflexive, that is no longer limited to the third-person singular in the present tense.

"I'm good" –
A standard response when asked "how are you?" You are not being asked about your moral state.

Never use slang when talking to partners or clients.

Formality

When meeting a client, partner or senior solicitor for the first time, start formally. Wear a jacket (and tie, in the case of men), call them "Mr" or "Ms" and observe the usual niceties – "How are you?", "Can I get you a tea/coffee?" and so on. After that, you can be guided by their express or implied behaviour. If they remove their jacket, you can remove yours. If they invite you to call them by their first name, do so. This is called "mirroring" and is very effective. You can cause unintended offense by being too informal too early but you are unlikely to cause offence by being formal initially. Older people require a little formality from others, particularly professionals, and will be happy, if they feel it is appropriate, to get you to lower your formality slightly.

Sloppy speech, mumbling and posture

You will have guessed by now that being a good solicitor can be as much about presentation as content. At the very least, clients expect you to be articulate and clear. It's why many bright students fail to impress. Keep the voice up (without shouting) and don't mumble. When you've said what you want to say, stop. Avoid the trap of filling silences with babble. Sloppy speech, mumbling and babbling annoys and confuses clients. Conversely, it's amazing the rubbish you can get away with if said with clarity, authority and confidence!

The same disciplined approach applies to posture. As

they say in the army, "don't slouch". You don't need to be a ramrod, but sloping head and shoulders is not a good look. Simply, stand straight and make good eye-contact.

Smartphones

A boon to humanity or curses of our age? The smart-phone has its uses, but switch it off and/or put it away when with clients. Glancing at your phone is as insulting as looking over your interlocutor's shoulder at a party to see if someone more important has turned up.

Drunk and disorderly

On qualifying in 1981, I joined Linklaters. At my first Christmas party, one trainee got so hammered he had to be carried out, Christ-like, on two colleagues' shoul-ders. Let's just say that his performance that night didn't enhance his career prospects. The moral: don't mix work and drink.

Office romances must also be handled carefully and sensitively. Mine created no problems, but office philan-dering, by men or women, is frowned upon, so be discreet. It can also help to be in a large firm: if the romance breaks down you're less likely to bump into your ex. On the other hand, it's not uncommon to meet the love of your life at work so don't be over-cautious.

Chapter 7
PHEW, YOU'VE MADE IT... AND NOW?

Should I stay or should I go?
You've come to the end of your training contract and you're a qualified solicitor. You may carry on with the firm where you trained. Or you may find yourself searching for a new firm, because you've been pushed out or want to leave, maybe to go in-house. Either way, you'll need to cope with a new set of challenges.

New job
If you are leaving, and applying to other firms, here are some basic interview rules:

1. Use all potential job sources, including employment agencies, internet adverts, personal or other connections. Narrow your search to specialism, location and firm size, but then keep it as wide as possible.

2. A little advance preparation works wonders. Find out about the firm and try to slip in a couple of questions during the interview that demonstrate that you've done your homework.

3. Follow my advice in chapter 5 about your appearance. Arrive early, offer a firm handshake and good eye contact, and don't fidget. It's all basic stuff but too easily forgotten.

4. Many people gabble when they're nervous. Consciously slow your delivery. It doesn't make you sound moronic.

5. Answer questions clearly and crisply. Then stop. Let the interviewer fill in any silences.

6. Think of a good, positive reason why you're leaving your current firm. Most interviewers will guess you've been "let go" but don't admit to this. Tell them you're looking for a smaller firm, more responsibilities etc. And never denigrate your current employer. It's unprofessional and suggests you might bad-mouth the new firm one day.

7. Follow any big stories in the legal world, and prepare something intelligent to say about them. When asked why you want to join their firm, flatter them without being unctuous.

8. Your interviewer may ask what salary you have in mind. Do not state a figure. You may pitch it too low, in which case you'll have blown a few thousand then and there. Too high, and they may think you arrogant. The best answer is "I'll leave it to you to come up with a figure" or something along those lines. What if the proposed salary is not mentioned in the interview but is specified in the subsequent written job offer? Should you ask for more? Probably yes, but be reasonable (i.e. no more than 10%). Most firms will find this acceptable behaviour. But do not ask for more if the proposed salary genuinely meets your expectations. Further salary discussions are best conducted by phone. Unless the proposed salary is derisory and assuming you want the job, I would, if pushed, graciously concede. At the very least, you've shown them you're not a soft touch and that you have some negotiating skills.

9. The job offer will contain other terms and conditions, e.g. working hours, benefits, non-compete covenants. Don't quibble for the sake of it. Only question them if you genuinely do not understand them and require clarification or if you have a real concern. These will be the firm's standard terms and conditions and are unlikely to change just for you. But do read them carefully so at least you know what you're letting yourself in for. You are, after all, a lawyer.

Change of status

The following applies whether or not you stay in your current job. On qualifying, you may think you're the bee's knees but to the partners and senior solicitors nothing much has changed in the way they see you, except that their expectations will be higher. Your salary will increase, you will be charged-out to clients at a higher rate, and you may be let loose on clients with less supervision than before. However, you still only have six months' experience in your specialism, and it may seem daunting. Have courage! You will grow into your new role. And until that time comes, put on a show of confidence and follow my rules on Bluffing and Questions, in Chapter 5.

Billing targets

I talked about timesheets previously. On qualifying, and for the rest of your career, you will be given a Billing Target which represents the amount you are expected to bill in the firm's financial year. It is normally pitched, depending on the firm and your level of experience, at three to four times your salary. You are not necessarily told explicitly about this target but you can be sure that the partners will focus on it.

You may or may not be told whether you have achieved your target but your continued existence in, and progress at, the firm are dependent on success in this area. More often than not, your failure to meet your target won't be your fault—there just won't be enough work or the person in charge of billing has written off some of your time. Not all firms take account of this when judging your performance. Remember, your role is to make large profits for the equity partners and they can be unforgiving. In addition, individual partners in your department may be criticised by other partners in the firm and they'll be reluctant to carry the can themselves. They may blame you expressly or tacitly.

Time bandits

Let's suppose your charge-out rate is £300 per hour. You've done five hours on the matter of Jones v Smith. Therefore, your Work-in-Progress (WIP) is £1,500. Other trainees' and solicitors' WIP on Jones v Smith is, say, £3,500 in total. So the total billable amount is £5,000 and the partner in charge has decided it's time to issue a bill. He will decide whether it is appropriate to increase or decrease that amount for billing purposes. And here comes the nasty bit. The partner has to apportion time spent by everyone on the matter for internal purposes. His figures are not looking so good and so he decides to attribute (i.e. take) your £1,500 and add it to his figure.

Partners or solicitors who do this are known as 'time bandits' but they'll get away with it. Consequently your billing figures will be lower and you may miss your billing targets. It's not all bad news. You may work on a matter where the partner is able to charge more than the WIP and so increases your share of that excess proportionately.

Bringing in business

Solicitors are divided into "Finders, Minders and Grinders". Finders bring in the clients, Minders look after them and Grinders do all the legal work. Most law firms think Finders are worth their weight in gold while Minders and Grinders are commonplace.

Finders were always important to a firm but in recent years they've become increasingly so and this trend is likely to continue, as law becomes more competitive. Increasingly cost-conscious clients rarely use a single law firm.

In short, if you are a proven Finder, the world is yours. By putting cash on the table you wield immense power. Having clients, and keeping them close to you, is called having "a following". Once you are above a certain level of seniority, you will be asked about your following at every interview—a decisive factor in deciding whether or not to hire you.

So the 64 million dollar question is how do you find new clients?

Luck:

This plays a big part. Family or friends may put business your way. They know what you do and they want to help you. Or a partner you work with retires and bequeaths you his clients, though you will have already done a fair bit of work for them and earned their trust.

Recommendation:

You have been seen in action and someone thinks you're good. It works with other professions, and being recommended is big feather in your cap.

Your little black book:

It's at times like these that you wish you'd been ruthless and careerist in the company you keep. You also need to be a great salesman, not something that lawyers are always good at. You phone your contacts and agree to meet for lunch or dinner or a social event and, after the appropriate chit-chat, you get to the point. This is an activity which should in theory carry on throughout your career. It's hit-and-miss and the odds are poor but you must grit your teeth and carry on. At the least, partners will ask you from time to time how your marketing is going and you need to show you're trying. In due course, you will need to produce results, but being seen to make an effort is better than nothing.

The right kind of friends:

A lot of our friends do well in large organisations but they are never in a position to decide which firm of lawyers their organisation should use. Friends who become entrepreneurs are best, though few people pick their friends like this. Some clients bring in minor work (e.g.

reviewing and modifying terms and conditions, drafting employment contracts, advising on small disputes etc.), but this doesn't normally generate enough money. Ideally, you want clients who are involved frequently in deals e.g. entrepreneurs, venture capitalists, private-equity mangers. If you generate over £150,000 - £200,000 a year, you will be taken seriously and those sort of clients could be your passport to future success at another firm.

Does all this sound like hard work? If you're lucky, it can happen smoothly and naturally. Unfortunately, increasingly, partners believe in the 'you eat what you kill' principle. If you can deliver a good following, you can play golf all day; nobody cares about your ability as a lawyer.

The two-year itch

After two years, you are able to work unsupervised. In short, you're starting to feel established, a true pro. At the same time, you are not too set in your ways. So, at this stage, you are very employable. A new firm feels that you would adapt well to their way of doing things. You see a lot of job adverts which fit the bill.

You may feel slightly restless. With tremendous discretion, start shopping around. Prospective employers will understand that you can only attend meetings early or late in the day. If you're not desperate to leave your current firm, you can afford to be choosy. And any offers will at the very least indicate if you're being adequately remunerated. But remember the grass isn't always greener.

Appraisals and salary reviews

Like Christmas, these come once a year. Some firms insist that there is no connection between appraisals and salary but I beg to differ. A good appraisal usually means a healthy salary increase and the opposite it also true. Every firm has its own approach to appraisals but it usually involves you filling a form about yourself before the appraisal meeting.

There's a balance to be struck here. You should be self-critical only up to the point you can foresee a solution, so be ready to discuss ways in which you can improve. Show willingness to work more and take on new responsibilities. In particular, think of things you can do to help the firm: e.g. join the know-how committee, write learned articles, etc. Listen intently to the partners' comments at your appraisal interview—vigorous nodding is recommended. Shortly after your appraisal, you should receive your salary review. At the very least, your salary should be increased in line with inflation. In addition, up until you are, say, seven or eight years qualified, it should be further increased to reflect your increased experience, higher charge-out rate and your improvement as a solicitor.

It is highly unlikely that any special pleading by you will improve the salary. You will have to consider whether it carries an unpleasant message, i.e. that it's time to go but you're not so bad that we need to fire you. Resist the temptation to confide in colleagues about your salary review as this can be dangerous and humiliating. Despite everything it may be that the firm is doing badly and cannot afford to pay more.

The good team player

You will find that in large organisations you work as part of a team. For example, in mergers and acquisition (M&A) work, this will probably be at least three members of the corporate department along with experts from employment, intellectual property and tax, for example, who will help with due diligence and related matters. If you're a solicitor in the corporate department, you may be effectively in charge of the transaction on a day to day basis.

You are like a rugby forward, the heaviest member of the scrum, who pushes the team forward inch by inch until it reaches the goal line. This involves a whole range of skills. Cajole rather than bully or threaten. Keep everyone informed of relevant progress. Ensure that every member of the team knows what he or she is supposed to do and by when. Never be disloyal to team members or land them in trouble. It's not a popularity contest but the other team members must like and respect you. In short, being in charge of a team will highlight your leadership qualities (or lack thereof). Your leadership skills will be scrutinised by the partners and will influence your promotion prospects.

Can leadership skills be taught? People go that extra mile because you have a special quality. There were certain partners at Lovells whose waste paper basket I would

gladly have emptied on a regular basis, not out of fear
(or interest in its contents) but because I wanted to please
them. Such leadership qualities will take you a long way.

Specialising

You will need to learn your chosen subject fast. Clients
and, to a lesser extent, partners will expect you to know
what you're talking about, and make very little allow-
ance for your lack of legal or commercial experience.
When drafting or reviewing documents, ask yourself
what commercial purpose they serve and how they all
fit together in the context of the transaction. To draft or
amend well, you need to understand your client's objec-
tives and what is important and what is minor in meeting
these. Where does the client want to end up at the end
of the transaction? Does your client want you to be a
Rottweiler and fight every point or adopt a more concili-
atory approach? What is the time scale? These are just
some of the questions you must ask yourself.

At the start of the transaction, you will need to know
which type of documents to use. Your starting point
is the firm's standard form precedents, then relevant
documents used by colleagues in similar transactions,
precedents in books, such as The *Encyclopaedia of Forms
and Precedents*, and finally, if none of the above fits the
bill, you will need to draft from scratch. The latter task is
one of the most intellectually stimulating parts of a solicitor's work and is also truly creative. I always find it best

to start with the "Defined Terms" and then go on to do skeleton clauses, but whatever works for you is fine.

The only people who will understand and sympathise with your lack of experience are colleagues. Get them to explain things to you. Ask them for precedents. Within reason, they will be happy to pass on their knowledge and experience. Reams have been written about negotiating skills and so I don't intend to write a small book on the subject here. But during your initial months of qualification this side of your abilities will be tested for the first time. Hardest of all is negotiation in person or by telephone because you do not have much time to think and respond. If you're stuck you can always use that hoary old legal chestnut, "I'll need to take my client's instructions on that". Don't get aggressive when you feel cornered or ignorant. Try to be on good terms with the other side's solicitor, but remain wary.

Talking things through with your client presents other difficulties. There may be moments when you don't understand what he wants or you don't know what the law or procedure is. Again be patient, don't lose your temper. And try not to bluff; if you give the wrong answer it could leave you in far bigger trouble. If you agree, or the client asks you, to do something by a certain time, make very sure that you do it. Do not disagree with advice given to him by colleagues or partners. Obviously, try to get on with the client, personal chemistry permitting. Always have to hand a good up to date text book (loose-leaf titles are best for this). Look up as regularly as you can websites which contain details of cases, statutes or other developments in your area, and email partners and colleagues about this whenever appropriate. On the commercial side, check the *Financial Times* regularly for developments. Perhaps most important of all, build up your own bank of precedents, always remembering that every transaction you work on is slightly different.

I cannot emphasise enough how important it is to hit the ground running in your chosen field. Partners and clients want to be able to trust you as soon as possible. Give them that confidence.

Going in-house

On qualifying some of you may decide that, for a variety of reasons, you no longer want to work in a law firm, and would prefer to go "in-house". That means being employed full-time by a company or other entity whose main business is not the law. They may have a legal department or just a single lawyer, from whom they take advice on a variety of legal matters. Although they may still use solicitors' firms for larger matters, the in-house legal department is nearly always the first port of call. Ultimately, it may save them money to have you there and it makes them feel they will get your full attention and input when they need it.

There are many advantages of going in-house. First, you will become more commercially aware and understand better the business climate in which your clients operate. Second, you will get to know a whole host of non-lawyers, which should broaden your horizons. Third, you will be exposed to a wider variety of work despite some of it being "farmed-out" to firms of solicitors. Finally, you will be free of timesheet pressures, bringing in new business and becoming a partner.

Of course, there are disadvantages. Although well paid, working in-house will not earn you the stratospheric incomes common for partners in a successful firm. Second, you will not be exposed to a variety of clients. Third, your employer may subtly—or not so subtly—pressure you into giving the opinion they want. You may not have the distance and objectivity which private practice allows.

Going in-house can be a finely balanced decision. However, there is another, perhaps the best, option but which is not within your control. You are temporarily "seconded" to one of your firm's clients, like a footballer out on loan. You can't be forced to go but you would be wise not to refuse. It will please both your firm and the client. You will gain in-house experience, while knowing that you will eventually return to your firm. And it allows you to cement relations between your firm and the client – i.e. being a "Minder" for your firm's business.

Partnership

In most cases, firms of solicitors are either partnerships formed under the Partnership Act 1890 ("Ordinary

Partnerships") or limited-liability partnerships formed under the Limited Liability Partnership Act 2000 ("LLP"). Most are Ordinary Partnerships but an increasing number are LLPs, particularly the larger firms. Whilst it has been possible for firms to operate as limited companies, few have done so, although the introduction of the Alternative Business Structure ("ABS") in 2010 may alter this. Ordinary Partnerships and LLPs are owned by the partners (also known as "equity partners"), each having a specified share of the business allocating to them the equivalent proportion of the firm's annual profit or loss.

The crucial difference between Ordinary Partnerships and LLPs—and the main reason why the latter have proved to be so popular—is that in Ordinary Partnerships each partner is jointly and severally personally liable whereas in an LLP each partner's personal liability is strictly limited as in a limited company.

Partners take their profit share by what are known as "Drawings". These are a monthly payment on account of that partner's profit share for the relevant year. If it turns out that a partner has drawn out more than his profit entitlement for that year, he must repay the excess to the partnership. If he has drawn out less, he gets a bonus.

Most partners will be required initially to make a capital contribution to the partnership and they should be able to recover this on leaving the partnership, either in one payment or by instalments.

Solicitors are required by the Solicitors Regulatory Authority (SRA) to take out insurance up to a certain level to meet potential negligence claims. Most firms take out still more insurance. So, although solicitors live in fear of enormous negligence claims, their potential personal liability is usually covered by "Professional Indemnity Insurance", i.e. insurance against negligence. Nevertheless some liabilities cannot be so readily covered by insurance, e.g. liability to their landlords, and this has resulted in a few firms "going under".

In the old days, a partnership share increased incrementally in accordance with age. This was known as the 'lock-step' system. Not anymore. There are now frequently unpleasant and divisive disputes among partners about their respective shares and profits. In well-regulated firms, the partnership is governed by a Partnership Agreement which covers such matters as capital contributions, voting rights, profit/loss, dissolution, retirement etc.

As well as equity partners, firms are increasingly appointing 'salaried partners' (something of a contradiction in terms), who get just a salary, have no say in the partnership's affairs and make no capital contribution. Salaried partners are held out to the world as a partner and are jointly and severally liable with the equity partners for the firm's debts and liabilities. In return, you receive an indemnity from the equity partners for those debts and liabilities.

That's the legal and commercial picture in very broad terms. Now let's consider some of the practical issues that arise when you become "partnership material".

1. In most firms you are considered for partnership when you are between five and 10 years qualified. It may be discussed or hinted at in appraisals or more informally. If nothing is forthcoming from the partners, you may have to "pop the question" yourself. If the response is negative or grudging, you would be well advised to start looking at other firms. Alternatively, the response may be positive but hedged around with Conditions—'work harder', 'bring in more business', 'show leadership skills', 'increase your billings'—and you must decide whether these stipulations are acceptable or even just an excuse to fob you off. The partnership dance is often slow and courtly and it may take a long time before you know where you stand.

2. Competition for partnership is like a horse race. The favourites are way out in front. Everyone knows who they are and they'll probably walk it. At the other end are the no-hopers. Most lawyers are somewhere in the middle. On a good day when conditions are favourable you may squeeze through. Some factors are totally outside your control, such as how well the firm is doing and how your department is faring and the nature of the competition in the relevant year. You will need a number of "supporters", partners who argue your case. You may know who they are but not how hard they pushed for you or how much influence they have.

3. Timing matters. Have you performed well in recent transactions, and if so did the more influential partners notice? Does your department need a new partner or partners in the relevant year?

For some solicitors, becoming a partner is the professional peak. The honour is enough in itself and they are less concerned about the terms offered. You, however, may scrutinise these. Is it salaried or equity? How much salary or what share of the equity? If salaried, ensure you get an indemnity from the other partners. What capital contribution will you have to make? These are all vital things to consider but very few solicitors turn down a partnership offer. At the very least, it is a stepping stone to something bigger and better.

Don't assume that becoming a partner will give you much say in how the partnership is run, though. "Magic Circle" firms, for example, have around 450 partners and, if you're one of them, you're unlikely to have much influence. There are always more rungs of the ladder to climb.

Phew, you've made it… and now?

So you'd like to be a lawyer?

ACKNOWLEDGEMENTS

This book would not exist without the generous help of Paul Lewis of Coptic Publishing, who believed in it and made it happen. Marc Lewis's witty illustrations add an extra sense of fun. Kate Gowrie's design is lovely.

Special thanks go to Sarah, for her love and support.

Lightning Source UK Ltd.
Milton Keynes UK
UKHW051806260319
339848UK00017B/505/P